RED VERSES

PEARLINA GRACELYN

Made with ♥ on the Notion Press Platform
www.notionpress.com

To every teen out there who thinks they're alone.

Contents

Contents

Preface

I can never declare that my poems are works of art that if not published, would be a loss to literature. My poems are nothing but life through the eyes of a teenage girl, presented in verse.

I yearn for people who have been through experiences like mine, to know that they are not alone. Teenage years are the hardest years of one's life, especially in today's world. I despise how teenage years are marketed as "the best years of one's life" . Well, no matter what, they aren't. I'm sure a bunch of you can agree there. You have been babied your whole life, and you strive hard to learn to walk as a toddler. In your teenage years, it feels like you're asked to swim when all you've been training for is to walk. This book isn't a book of poetry. It is going to be a bunch of episodes in my life, expressed in the way I know best. Before the beginning of most poems, a context and the premises for the writing, will be provided for understanding, which may help one to relate. I hope you like it. More power to you! ♡

Most of my writings have dark themes and resolutions which I do not condone in any way, nor have I practised them. Writing is my sole way of expressing my anger and the dark thoughts which reign over my head. Everybody has intrusive thoughts, and these are mine. These are only for one to find relatability, not ideas ;)

(Note that, some of the poems make use of small letters only. This is to showcase raw vulnerability in contrast to a formal and polished one, which may seem impersonal.)

Acknowledgements

Firstly, I thank God for blessing me with the passion to write. I thank Him alone for enabling me to bring out fruitfulness from my times of trial.

I thank Dr. Samuel Rufus, who has been my guide and mentor. Without his motivation and encouragement, this project would not have been possible.

I thank Megha Sumesh, who proofread the entire book, with utmost cheerfulness.

I thank Catherine Jasper, who brought my vision to light with a wonderful cover page. For more of her exquisite designs, you can check out @charlotte_pourquoi on Instagram

And last but not the least, thank you. You are the reason I write. Thank you for all the ways you've inspired me, knowingly or unknowingly. I'm eternally grateful!♡

"The courage to love in this mortal and ever fleeting world is something to be celebrated"

1. Resentment

Hmm, well there are many reasons for this being the first poem of this book. I wouldn't say it's my favourite. However, it definitely does stand out. I remember where I was when I wrote this, which pen I used, and how relieved I felt after getting such disturbing emotions on paper. This is one of the first poems I've written. I was being taken advantage of, and I could put up with it no more. Standing up for yourself is so much more difficult than letting yourself be taken advantage of. That's a hard pill to swallow. But it's true, and might resonate with most of us. When I realised just how much people around me were using me, it wasn't just hurt or sadness. It was resentment. Much much resentment, which, of course, a couple years later I did get my apologies. However the feeling I felt as a lonely 11th grader still stings.

1. Resentment
As I go through each memory,
I feel a stroke of chivalry.
Left for the right reasons,
Because of all the treason.
Although I'm shattered to pieces,
Never again will I let myself be exploited,
By somebody who's clearly demented.
I feel disappointed and defeated,
For the way I let myself be treated.
No, no, and a million times no,
No more will I let you feel superiority,
No, you don't have any authority,
Not anymore, no.
You regret it don't you?
Well I sure hope you do.
I anticipate your repentance,
Drowned in embarrassment.
Would savour every bit of it,
You better make the most of it.
Don't you dare count on its acceptance,
All it gives me is sustenance.
Well I don't wish the best for you.
I hope you learn what it's like to be on the other side,
And feel pure remorse every waking moment
because you deserve it, honey
All the things you did to me.
I abhor you
And it's all thanks to you.

2. Queen Bee

Ah yes, the queen bee. When reading the title, she pops into your head doesn't she? Well this poem is a continuation of "Resentment". Although "Resentment" wasn't written for the alleged Queen Bee, she was, definitely, one of the main reasons. You know when life's going perfectly fine, and an angel knocks at your door, which was a curse in disguise? Yes! That was queen bee to me. The best way in my experience to deal with such people, is to simply exit the situation and pray for them in secret.

2. Queen bee
Although I should be
I'm not in the least surprised.
You desired my belonging,
It worked out for you
Oh so beautifully.
You saw that it had holes,
Like that of a honeycomb's,
You had to be the queen bee,
Otherwise it didn't feel free.
Tore each apart didn't you?
Slowly but gently,
Whilst assuring me,
Guaranteed, I'm clumsy.
To shed light on your little kingdom,
I implore you, possess at least a puny amount of wisdom ,
To realise this is not envy,
I would rather burn, than posses that plenty.
I turn around and, Oh
You sting slowly but carefully,
I'm truly perplexed by this double crossing,
Did thy not conclude that my possession was indeed poisonous ?
Well you did provide shelter when needed,
Was that also a loophole to steal?
It looks so.
Was warned by the drones,
Still chose to sow.
Your fate won't be death,
T'will be worse than you could imagine,

With that big but disgusting head of yours.

Above all a true power stands,

Watching over your offence,

And He won't go in silence.

You chose to be a traitor,

To a speck in the galaxy,

That's all I was and will ever be.

3. Who would've thought?

I used to be a loner. I had very few friends and I was happy with that. I barely even spoke to anyone. However, in a surprising turn of events, I got into a sticky situation with the so called 'popular' kids, which prompted me to write "Resentment" and "Queen Bee". After getting out of that situation, I was suddenly clueless as to who I was. I'm used to being unheard, unnoticed, unseen. Suddenly it was my name that came out of everyone's mouth. I didn't like it. I had no wish to be heard, noticed and seen. Who would've thought this would happen to me? Life is hilarious sometimes.

3. Who would've thought

Who would've thought

That I, the unnoticed,

The one to whom you wouldn't pass another look,

Would get stuck with the admired,

And is dying for a way out.

Who would've thought

That I, of all people, could fetch the 'best'?

Well it happens to be the worst.

It left scars,

Taught me things I shouldn't know.

Every part of me

Is lost in the galaxy.

Who am I? Who is she?

I don't know anymore.

All that happened to me, the silenced

The dumbfounded, the isolated

Who would've thought?

4. My Discomposure

Although I got myself out of those sticky situations, I was still as broken as I would've been if I hadn't. The aftermath of everything was somehow more cruel than going through it. I was somehow able to get a grasp on how toxic relationships work through this experience. As much as it hurts, one would rather go back than be free. It's beautiful how pain teaches one so much about life. Pain is evidence that one is alive. But one must never decide not to do something due to the fear of pain. Fear of pain is like fearing the next breath you take. Pain and joy, both come and go, and will come and go throughout your life. Refrain from being scared of your life, and try to welcome each possibility each day, no matter what. God has beautifully written your life and has plans to prosper you. Pain is only shaping you to be a better person. Therefore, never, ever fear pain.

4. My discomposure

Why does it ache so much?

Why do I care?

I felt peace in my hatred,

Now I'm drowned in sentiment.

I had true notions after all,

Pretty sure that makes one of us.

As much as I'm wounded,

I'd rather be absconded

than to have any connection with thy.

One might say it's pride

But I say it's protection

From the words which strike.

I hide behind every excuse,

to save the last bit of my wrecked soul.

Now it doesn't matter anymore.

I'm done once and for all,

Or so I think.

I should return the gifts given to me

Such as overthinking

Depression, and well,

Soon enough, you'll get them.

5. Confessions

Well, in the poems before, all I've been talking about is what other people did to me, who they were and how they broke me and so on. Now it's time to talk about me. I was never a saint, nor have I proclaimed to be. Nobody can be a saint too. It is important to always acknowledge where you go wrong. But I sometimes went down a rabbit hole where I always thought I was in the wrong. It's important to have confidence in your conduct as well as apologise with utmost humility when you err. Another idea conveyed through this poem is how no matter what a person is going through, their conduct toward you is not an expectation but rather a necessity. Yes I was dealing with a broken heart, but that gives me no right to lash out on my friends. I wrote this poem to someone who I hurt. I wrote this as an apology which, to my joy, was well received.

5. Confessions

These are those confessions,

Of multiple transgressions.

Which I performed under commission.

I believed I deserved execution,

But it was instead a realisation.

A reality check, a wake-up call,

For which I screamed out to the Lord.

He told me to confess,

Nevertheless, it gave me distress.

The misery, sorrow, and gloom

Isn't an excuse.

On a random afternoon

I decided to go through each tomb,

Hoping it wouldn't be my doom.

I believe I've found peace,

Never in my dreams did I imagine

That one could be so humble,

So pure, so giving,

So understanding, so loving.

I'm talking about my best friend,

Who I got closer to because of a confession.

6. Unheard

I ended "Queen Bee" with the lines "a speck in the galaxy, that's all i was and will ever be." Until recently, I've always had the habit of belittling myself. I've felt like a cloud in the sky, a ripple in the ocean, or a hair on the head. These things could go missing, and no one would notice. This is the sole reason why I took to writing. The pages knew me better than my peers, thus I felt at home with them. Speaking was never my forte. I was unheard. I remember a classmate saying that the day I opened my mouth, there would be cyclones. Ironically though, for someone unheard, I had a lot to say.

6. Unheard

To always be perceived as dumbfounded,

Is beginning to crush my foundation.

To always be thought of as timid,

It'll never be a merit.

The fear in my heart, soul, and mind,

To all of them, you'll turn a blind eye.

What if I wake up and she's gone?

The future is my biggest unease

You don't understand,

I see visions of being abandoned,

Dreams filled with regret,

A trio left to eternity.

How do I know that this won't too?

I know I'm being dramatic in your eyes

"Think positive," they say,

Just how easy do they think it is?

I'm holding on to the bits and pieces

Hoping to find sustenance.

7. Cherished

To add onto more context for the last poem, my family was deeply affected by COVID, which led to the death of three of my family members. My dad, my grandpa and my grandmother- my best friend. Downsizing from a house of seven to four, isn't easy at all, even now. Since the three deaths took place in a span of six months, I have been living in paranoia, wondering who death will knock at next. Losing family members are permanent scars, which leave innumerable questions. The only hope which keeps me going, is that God himself will answer my questions someday. I thank Him alone for leading my family and I thus far.

The next few poems are all about how I felt losing my beloved family.

7. Cherished

When tomorrow starts without you,
Oh, I cannot imagine how it would do,
I cannot go a minute without you,
How will an eternity do?
I cherished every moment with you,
and I would've cherished it more,
but you went without a warning
and it disheartens me every morning.
I'd like to believe that we'd meet again,
that's the only thing I anticipate
when I look up at the heavens above,
I imagine your warm smile as I see that dove,
flying away in freedom,
with pure joy and serenity,
giving me clarity.
Although my heart is heavy,
I know you're happy,
and that's all that matters to me,
as time hopefully fixes me.

Chapter8

If my dreams are the only place where you're seen,
Then I wish to never wake up.
If I can retain only one thing in my memory,
I'd forget everything to remember you.
If you said come along and pointed to a dark valley,
I'd jump in without hesitance.
I'd give up anything,
My life,
My dignity,
My arrogance, or whatever it takes
To have just a glimpse of you.
The void in my heart is humongous,
Words cannot describe its proximity.
I keep trying to fill it in the wrong places
Nothing brings me joy or peace anymore.
I don't see the point if it's not you.
Although life doesn't breathe in you anymore,
You are full of delight in my head,
A marvellous sight for one to see
I wish to keep dreaming and keep pondering upon you,
I wish to never be awake or to have my eyes open, ever.
Because you've expired according to the Earth

9. Those Days

Those were the days,
Days of cheer and laughter
Days with my grandparents and dad,
And of course, my favourite uncle who was also my pastor
Those were the days
Those were the days,
When I filled my days
With endless complaints
How stupid, ungrateful was I,
I didn't realise that time would pass by, so fast
Those days
Those were the days,
When I could sleep at nights still
Where my problems weren't chronic
Nor was my heart throbbing
With fear each beginning
Those were the days
These are the days,
Where I don't complain, at all
Although I've lost it all
The irony of it all
When each waking moment,
Feels oh so violent
Those were good days

Chapter10

It's black and evil
Take it off, you scoundrel
A robe filled with elephants and turtles
You'll be of disposal
Throw it and wash yourself
It might mean mountains to you
But you cannot be accepted if you put it to use
It means more than mountains to me
The robe paints my world
Covers me while walking through the dark
Protects me when evildoers come upon me
Disposing of it would be of disaster
I won't be able to recover
my beloved grandmother
Flying above the heavens
watching me, with a bright smile
and present as my guardian angel
maybe it's all in my head
maybe it's the reason for all the misery
I'll take it off and keep it safe
in my bowl of memories
making it history

11. 2021

Well, those 6 poems sum up my life during 2021. Although it was such a scarring year, at the end of it I was reminded to be grateful, and the Lord gave me a spirit of thanksgiving for the year. I was hopeful for what would happen next.

11. 2021

Injures and scars,

Imprinted on arms,

An eventful journey ends,

As the melancholic sunsets.

I thank the Creator

For being the leader

And forever the centre.

He allowed me to encounter such,

Expanding my views much.

With a new vision

And new eyes,

I'm beyond thrilled for the new beginning,

Which is hopefully filled with singing.

Even if it happens to be the same,

I'm afraid I won't go lame.

I won't let myself be framed.

2021 made me tame.

12. 2022

Ah, time for the year of absolute embarrassment. To cope with all that happened in 2021, I made some decisions in 2022. And to put it lightly, they were not pretty. This is a poem that I wrote on 31st December 2022. So, here are some spoilers.

12. 2022

The world seems pretty,
Like the old apple falling from the tree.
It indeed tests me,
I wanna pick that up and treat me.
I've always been pretty holy,
It's time to let loose and folly,
To feel the highs and lows and get the jollies.
The bliss of every night,
The reality of every morning,
The hungover which sticks throughout the week.
I was there for every bit of the mourning,
Endless possibilities I seeked.
Failure or success doesn't matter.
If I could turn back time I would still falter.
If I went back to the spring,
I wouldn't change a thing.
I rejoiced the highs,
Voiced out the lows,
Coexisted with the love and misery,
Got a couple of enemies.
My skills dazzled like melodies
What a year, has it been
2022, helped me win.

13. Drugs

I was someone brought up with beautiful christian values, which I as a very 'play by the rules' kid, have never faltered about. This good girl image of me completely tarnished after the death of my family members. I've always been good, played by the rules, and obedient as much as I can. To still be struck by lightning left and right, was unacceptable to me. I finally decided to let loose. I wanted the world and all of its disguised beauty. I wanted it for its darkness and to dwell among it. I can confidently say that that was the dumbest decision I've taken, for life has taught me over and over, that true joy can be found only in the Lord. The world can never satisfy. However, once again through more pain, I was able to learn more about myself and life. Here is a poem and an essay about this very dilemma in my mind.

13. Drugs

The long thin tiny needles,

Stuck in my nerves since birth.

Into it flows some substance,

Which gives me all the high

And blurs all the life.

It's intoxicating, numbing,

Without them it's freeing.

The scars on my nerves are healing,

But for some reason, I still hover.

Closer to the fire,

Closer to that sharp knife,

That my mother told I wasn't allowed to play with.

That burning flame looks more dangerous than ever,

Might as well go put my hand in it.

14. Rules

All my life, I've been told to play by the rules. The rules were surprisingly easy to fit in though, because I was just a child and I matured pretty late. I was friends with similar people, so I wasn't introduced to the world. Hence playing by the rules was easy. It was something that was natural. Even though I grew up in an abusive environment, playing by the rules meant playing life right. But slowly, as I grew up, I paid attention to myself more and to my heart more. No longer did I hear my house, my parents, I heard just my heart. Not even my brain, which seemed to speak sense. I wanted fun. I wanted to break the barriers. I wanted to let loose. I was tired of being the good innocent girl. After being exposed to the beauty that is in the world, I wanted all of it too.

Chapter15

Growing up,
Is like untying knots.
It's like you've always had this rope,
And day by day,
Lesson by lesson, you start noticing where it's tied.
Untying it will be hard, as we all know, old habits die hard.
But if taken gently, and untied with utmost patience,
It makes a lasting impact.
Untying makes the rope longer,
As when you put off unhealthy habits, life does seem longer.
In a good way of course.
Things, thoughts, people.
That used to bother and rue the day, Seem childish to one with good
ways

16. What is Love?

Well, the last few pieces make it seem like I became a wretch in 2022. It did feel like that then, but looking back at it now, not so much. I am able to understand the dire situation I was in, and sympathise with myself completely. However, in that moment, I was drowned in regret and loathed every bit of me. T'is always beautiful to connect with your past self. To love someone, means to love every version of them, even their past self. One cannot just love who one is now and call it love. When we take so much consideration in how to love someone, how much more must we take to love ourselves! Take this as your opportunity to forgive yourself, and fall in love with yourself. This was a poem I wrote for someone who I thought would last forever. Crazy how teenage ideas work. Of course it didn't, it didn't last even for a year, and left my broken self even more broken.

16. What is Love?
No one told me
That this is how it should be.
This is how it is to be happy,
And this is how love should make one feel.
I thought what I had
Was delightful and beloved,
But indeed it was pain and hunger,
Yearn and tears was what love had to be.
"Starving people will eat anything," they say.
If only I knew I was starving while being fed,
If only I stopped believing that
"Love is pain".
But you taught me, so patiently
Love is joy,
Love is life,
Love is everything,
We are called to one another, what a joy.
You removed my fears;
You were patient,
You were kind,
Oh I see, love is kind.
The feeling of being alone
Is so much worse than fearing love.
It's better to have loved and lost indeed,
Because that so-called love has made me who I am,
And you seem to love who I am.
Birthgivers and blood relations showed me their "love",
It would be better to call it abuse.

Still, you chose to love every broken piece of me.

And walked your way into my heart,

Like it was so easy.

You speak with such a perfect cadence,

The way you look at me, someone pinch me

My future was scary, but now it's all sparkly

I cannot stop smiling.

17. My Wedding Day

17. My Wedding Day
I woke up this morning
With a joy unconcealing,
My mouth wider than ever, blushing,
The day is finally arriving.
The day I finally, officially marry
The most loving, caring, supporting.
Oh, I could keep going.
Jesus, am I dreaming?
Looking back at our childhood,
How beautiful was our love,
All of our phone calls,
All the times we secretly looked at each other.
Then, as we parted ways for further education,
It took a lot of dedication
But we made it so easy,
We were both firm in forever,
All our video calls and texts, I cherish forever,
Now as I'm standing in front of you,
The love of my life, with tears of joy,
I release a sigh of relief, that we've finally made it
Although I'm not surprised at all.
You look at me and say "I do"
I cry with overwhelming joy,
You take my hand and we walk through the aisle,

As husband and wife.

Chapter18

Now, fast forwarding a bit into the future, I had just joined college. College was extremely difficult to adjust to. I had just lost bonds with 3 people, with whom I thought it would last forever. However, I was healing. I was slowly learning everything around me, and maturing as the Lord beautifully led me. I was beginning to get an idea of what love was actually supposed to be. But still, as they say old habits die hard, it was difficult for me to break out of the pattern of masochism. However, I tried and kept trying. All that glitters is not gold. I know that better than anything now., If you feel like it's impossible for you to break out of toxic cycles, believe me, it's not. It takes a lot of work, but if you're ready to put in the effort, you can. It will be painful to walk away from things that usually seem shiny and colourful, but the day you realise that it was just a lump of coal, congratulations, you've healed.

18.

I keep telling myself I don't like you.

It's in hopes that that feeling would eventually fade away.

The feeling I get when I watch you walk through any door in the world,

it lifts my face with a beaming smile.

The feeling when you talk to me,

I feel like the only beautiful woman to exist in the world.

The feeling when you laugh because of my jokes,

Gosh I hope that all of your laughs and all of your smiles

have a sliver of me as the reason.

The feeling when you talk to other women,

one which makes me want to jump into a pool of fire and cry,

I hide it with an innocent smile.

The feeling when you came forward and called me, and told it's time to go.

The feeling that you remembered me, nothing could beat that.

The feeling when I saw you watch my every move as I danced,

I would train myself to the bone,

if it meant you'd be the audience.

The feeling when you told me you liked me,

followed by the masochistic joy when I told you no.

The feeling when you told me all that we could've been and

The feeling when i think of the painting of our future, one which i painted meticulously,

torn apart to shreds by the same old me.

I keep telling myself that I don't like you.

it's in hopes that these feelings would eventually fade away.

19. To the Love of my Life

19. To the Love of My Life
I think about you from time to time
What will it be like?
Will I know the importance of you?
The second I meet you?
Or will you be like a passing cloud,
That makes its comeback
Just when I think it's all over?
Do you even exist,
Or does my God expect me
To carry on my solidarity?
Oh how I long for your reality.
Spare me out of my misery,
Love me the way I should've been.
Look into my eyes, don't let them wander,
For the rest of your world, blurs at the sight of me.
For that's how much you love me.
You would truly understand what I mean
And not lash at my flow of speech.
You would comprehend my wildest fantasies
And behold me as your dearly.
I mistook you to be someone else
and let you down,
Now my loyalty is devoted to you only.
Please love the Lord, more than you'd love me,

And come to reality as we speak.
I miss you dearly, my love.
Make the first move at once,
Let's join hands in love
and seek the one above.

20. The Backstory

So what happened to me in 2022? As I had already mentioned earlier, I've always been a play by the rules goody two shoes. When I lost my family members and went through a number of other things during quarantine, I realised that playing by the rules had gotten me nowhere. So I decided to do whatever I want, which now I realise was absolute foolishness. Instead of cherishing the values I was brought up with, I deserted them with joy. I looked for love elsewhere. Looking for love and the want to be loved is beautiful, but it is so important to know what exactly you're looking for. Love means different things to different people. To find like minded people is extremely difficult in this world. My best friends and I have such different views on life. That is completely fine. But when one is choosing a partner, someone to spend the rest of one's life with, it is extremely important to share the same value system. As a Christian, I believe that there are three people in every relationship. You, your partner and God. Now do you see how important it is for me to find someone who loves the Lord like me? Loving someone who doesn't would be useless. When your beliefs don't coincide, it is going to end in heartbreak. And after going through one, I don't think I'll ever voluntarily put myself through such excruciating pain ever again. This is why dating culture and casual relationships puzzle me. How one can just turn off their emotions in getting involved with someone, I'll never know, and honestly don't want to. Although the one I chose to love in 2022 was someone who did share the same values, I think it's safe to say that it ended in shambles. I am not here to blame the other party or myself or the circumstances. It simply wasn't meant to be. Although I do firmly believe that the other party could've dealt with it so much better, I have matured enough to take it as a learning experience, and through the grace of God, have learned to forgive. I kept this relationship a secret, and to put it lightly, my close confidants were not pleased. This led to my friendships also being hampered, and the cherry on top was a secret love affair, which chose to announce itself at the worst possible time. My house was also pretty chaotic, and I went through all of this alone, just whispering prayers to God here and there.

Starving people will eat anything. Remember that. Make sure that any type of relationship around you is only helping you grow. No friendship or relationship of any sort should be the centre of your life. They only add to your life. You do not need to beg anyone or anything to stay with you, to live your life. Your life is your own, a gift from God. God has not made you to only be able to cherish that gift with someone else. It is your own, meaning this gift was packaged and addressed only to you. Therefore, take pride in your independence and admire yourself in joy, with the knowledge that the Lord who created the universe knows you by your name, loves you and will never ever leave you.

The next couple poems are poems written during the darkest nights of my life yet (I hope). I'd like to think of them as my best work, and I hope it helps you too.

Chapter21

i'm a sole lone robot
in this world of mozarts.
I rise day by day and do my duties
with no reaction whatsoever to anything.
but today is different.
I suffered a malfunction.
now all i can do is think of
wisdomous and wrangly things of sorts.
it won't shut down, it keeps going on,
oh why did i ever complain of being a robot

22. drowning

22. drowning
as i fall deep into the river,
my life flashes and hovers
a mother who's never happy,
tears every morrow she reaps.
a sibling who's in too deep,
and she lets her teeth sink
and flies with dramatic wings.
i drown myself in my phone,
because nothing can be done to swim ashore.
friends and love i find,
many lend a hand and ask to dance.
the consuming void left by dad,
slowly began to repair,
or so i thought.
they suddenly don't wanna dance with me no more
an unexpected proposal floored up
a kiss i can't wait to wash off,
the last dance i can't stop thinking of,
so i jumped in the river
drowning myself with poetry and math
choosing the things none could beware
just so it would help me drown and dissolve
because i can't face this world, not at all.

Chapter23

A heart so thine and tender
Goes out in search in this stormy weather
She seeks lust and vengeance in her lair
I watch her dig her own graveyard
Who am I to stop her?
Lust she seeked and lust she found
For every hidden soul is alas in unison to a seeker
Like how the early morning skies and the darkness of hell
Have quite a bit of similarity with them, if you will
They both signify doom
They also, despise each other
Thus the lust consumes thy tender heart
It devours the innocence ever beheld
The early morning skies, soon evolves into the dead of night
And all that's left of me, is a sigh, from being the spectator
And of course, a heavy, devoured heart.

24. to be honest

24. to be honest
to be honest
i wish i had my bestfriend
i wish she never left
i wish we never grew apart
i wish we were still the sisters i've always dreamt of
to be honest
i wish the crowd still asks us
"where's the other one?"
i wish we're still the duo
that everyone wishes they were
i don't mean to sound too shallow
just being honest
to be honest
i wish i still had my boyfriend
no matter what it was
i loved him that i'd crush my flower vase
dip my hands in the glass
squeeze every drop of blood and bone
to see if that would make him love and hope
for me and no one else but me
to be honest
i wish my best friend didn't love me
i wish he was just my best friend
i wish he was my wingman

i wish he'd find his princess
who'd make him so happy
oh it would be priceless
to be honest
i wish i could forget more
funny how i forget everything
but remember my dads yelling voice
and my mother's squeal
as dad squeezes her throat
how i hid under my own clothes
as i heard dad lock mom in a room
and my mom thumping on the door
in worry and fear
to be honest
i'm only living for Jesus
i can't wait for all this to end
that i'll be on my way
to eternity, oh can't wait for that day
just being honest

25. on the other side

25. on the other side
why don't the books and movies
ever talk about how i'm feeling?
people like me are painted wrong
and everyone who watches them,
pray for our befall
do you know what it's like on the other side?
everyone would side with you,
say that the rejected is the one with excruciating pain.
but do you know what it's like to reject?
to truly let down someone who you love?
to be the reason of their sadness,
to put yourself first, and realise,
nothing will be the same again.
i watch you distance from me
and i can't blame you, nor will i
i never thought you'd say goodbye
and i blink away tears at the sudden change
the change of pace i notice
at the start of every minute.
for your peace of mind, you push me away.
i thought this was the perfect friendship,
only to realise it was so,
because one of us was in love.
and i also failed to realise,

that as you fall out of love,
the friendship isn't so perfect,
and you don't even understand why i'm sad,
because it only makes sense for you to be,
god it sucks to be on the other side.
i thought no one could replace you.
i didn't find joy in my moments,
if i didn't share them with you and laugh about it.
that's how much this friendship meant to me.
you're teaching me that this friendship meant nothing to you.
you either wanted me as a lover
or out of the picture.
well that's pretty cool;
the new friends i'm making
are slowly filling the void you left aching,
and eh i guess
i'll be okay on the other side.

Chapter26

how is it that it's always me
left behind in the grasses,
scrounging for coins and
i wish i could set things up for me
for i hate being an anomaly.
God so help me
everytime i look at you and smile with my teeth
indeed i wonder how to close the greet
i abhor you with reasons you couldn't imagine
if only the world was my door handle.
a family is a blessing,
friends are a bounty,
both of which i am void.
thus is the Lord's choice.

Chapter27

i was looking up at the stars,
when you told me you'll never pass me by;
that you'll hold my hand,
and fill every void.
i was looking up at the stars,
when you told me i was the only one;
that you will make me see the sun,
for it has been so long,
i had forgotten it's touch.
i look up at the stars,
and think of the lies which seemed so true;
with every blink a little tear
i look up at the stars.

Chapter28

you seem to be happy
your teeth all crispy and shiny
in those pictures which i hate to see.
you're not allowed to be happy.
you make me second guess my being;
how can you even forget,
days of texts and smiles
conversations that opened minds
you walked away without a goodbye
everytime i think i'm fine
you give me a reason to die
well at least there i'd be in joy
for the Lord's love is divine.

Chapter29

i cannot wait to cut contact with you,
to tear apart every last sliver of you,
for it is so easy for me to forget,
things of such trivial importance.
the time i make money, the time i age,
i would smile so wide as i would be free.
free from having to abide in the same abode as your being;
with my smile so wide i bite out the chains
which stuck me to you all along.
blood, is just another liquid,
that doesn't mean we'll make it to the finish.
every breath away from you
would feel oh so liberating,
i await the day, i await the feeling,
shaking with tears
with cuts on my arms
i write this to you
just incase i don't make it
know that i've always and always
hated.

Chapter30

a perfect picture if i ever took one

in hopes to still the ever fleeting time

almost seems like a fish impossible to catch

it keeps swimming and away it goes

lost in the ripples of my tears

the sound of the wind in my ears

blocks you out of my mind

the ringing sound of your agony

caused by all my blasphemy

piece by piece

little by little

memory by memory

i let go of the fish i caught

somehow, it has been a year since i've seen it

how i wish that i hadn't caught it again

Chapter31

the nights are when i'm at my weakest
even the sound of a water drop
can sound like that of a screaming woman
or cries of help for rescue
from someone or something just too scary to even pen down.
you say you love me
you say you care
hell, you even show it through actions
or wait.. you just talk to me more..i don't know if that counts as actions
anyway, i thought you'd be there with me
during the nights
not holding my hands when i shudder
or wiping my tears during every wail,
nor assuring me it'll be okay;
and not even looking at me,
just.. i thought you'd be there
here. in this room. with me.
you don't even have to pay attention to me
all you had to do
was be there.
but you never were
never are
never will be

Chapter32

finally got around cleaning up the mess i made
why did i put it off so long?
maybe because having that mess around
felt like i still had pieces of you.
i didn't have the guts to realise
that they were actually pieces of me, not you.
you left forever ago;
every fragment of me holds a memory of you.
I can have memories of you, sure,
but not this close to my heart.
not like before.
I thought it was already clean,
but all i did was put a towel over it
and i dropped bits here and there,
everywhere i went.
Now i'm following back my trail,
cleaning up the mess i made,
thinking i was ready,
thinking im alright.
But i watch as every sweep
and every mop
the cleaner it gets
the clearer you become.
that's when i realise
i can drink myself numb,

i can wipe off every speck,

but you my love,

will always live rent free in my head.

mess or mess free,

you've always got a place here.

Chapter33

I'm a sound person;

I use words for which I don't know the meaning of,

wherever it sounds right.

I stare with dead eyes into my music book,

Making it look like i'm reading the notes.

In reality my hands tremble,

waiting for instructions from my ears,

For I can play the piece only with the sounds I've heard;

It's the only way I know how.

Im a sound person;

When I enter a room with sounds of roaring laughter,

I listen intuitively to the type of jokes

And pretend to be one among them.

I add my own at ease,

and become a part of the room.

When I hear my favourite cartoon come on,

I leave everything at once,

drowning my ears with all the nostalgia

and the tunes of the simpler times.

I'm a sound person;

Whenever I hear my parents fight

Or my sister scream

or my uncle cry,

I drown it out

with tears and sounds of my own.

When I heard my best friend say
That she doesn't know me anymore,
Or the guy who I thought id marry say
That I'm just not worth it,
I decided to not be a sound person,
rather be one with a vision.
A vision to discern between good and bad,
A vision to love even more than before,
A vision to have my own family,
A vision to never settle,
And most importantly, a vision to have my own people
who take me back to who I am,
A sound person.

34. Metro Rides

34. Metro Rides
even though the days began with tears,
or the world seemed like it would end,
everyday i would take
these metro rides.
even when you told me you loved me,
you wished to marry me,
i walked to this station
and took a metro ride.
when you broke my heart,
for someone half your age,
i sat in the metro,
talking to myself through the ride.
be it when i was 18 and happy,
or 17 and suicidal,
i always sat right here,
the seat next to the trash can,
taking a metro ride.
i'd complain so hard,
to strangers who'd rather be damned;
i'd close my eyes and lean,
dreaming of a time you'd be damned.
but these metro rides,
which always arrived just before a minute;
these random people around me,

who watched me lose my patience;
they've become a routine,
and now that it's the end of the beginning.
i'll have to go without a metro ride for a while.

Chapter35

suddenly i realise
all my efforts are in vain
all this running away
has stirred up to be
pointless.
i've become you
it's in my nature;
it clearly runs in my blood,
and it no longer shows just in my height
or my colour.
it's in the way i talk,
the way i defend my mother;
the way i show my wrath,
i almost began to sympathise with you.
what happened to you?
being the big, monstrous creature
that none could comprehend?
what happened to you?
being the reason for all my misery
the reason i wished to die.
now with the remaining pieces in my head
which is all i have since you're dead
all i can see when i think of you
is me.

Chapter36

tied to a pole,

sitting all alone;

barren bones,

and a drooling tongue.

you may have much to complain,

much to cry for,

wonder when you'll eat again,

wonder when you'll be free to run,

when you're thirst will be quenched,

when the guard's whips,

will come to a halt.

and yet you smile,

you stand up on your feeble feet.

so fragile, that it may break when touched.

you wag your tail, in joy,

not just for me,

but for everyone who passes by,

even the guard.

you're a constant reminder

of how much i need the saviour;

how dare i grumble

when i have all you need?

how dare i want more

than good food and a home?

how dare i have the guts,

to even desire
a better ending?
true i may have lost it all;
but my worst,
is the best he'll ever have.

37. Friday 9:51 PM

37. Friday 9:51 PM
Every year, every month, everyday
Every hour, every minute, every second
Through every breath, blink and bite
I am stuck in a loop, trying to forget.
Raindrops on roses,
Whiskers on the four of my kittens,
Be it a speck of dust, or a frame tilted wrong,
You manage to infiltrate all.
You're a movie telecasted everywhere,
You've landed in the lips of people who don't even know you;
If such is your power from a distance,
Your power over me must've been immeasurable.
Thanks to everything you affirmed on that Friday,
I gave all of myself away.
Your rule over me was torture,
And all I had to comfort my heart
Were the words you told me at 9:51.
I took pride in being your favourite slave,
I even begged you for a leash.
If that's not pathetic enough, this will be;
That I, even now
After all the storms have passed, farms watered, and flowers sprung,
The only reason i have for a grin
Is the ever fading memory

of the words you told me, on that Friday at 9:51PM

And how if they were true,

I would be doomed.

• 61 •

38. To My Classmate

38. To My Classmate
"someday i'll get over you"
was what i always used to say
whenever you spoke to me,
looked at me,
smiled at me,
it took everything in me, and more
in order to not do the same.
Whenever you speak to me
it takes the strength of God
for me to not tell you about my whole life,
every little detail,
listen, watch your reaction,
laugh with you
and have everything like it was before.
instead i have to settle to a nod;
a nod and a mere smile, yeah that's all i do and can do,
for you've made it clear you don't wanna go there again.
you would like to remain mere classmates.
i'm sorry but that's impossible;
you were my all. my everything. when i think 'friends', i think you.
you defined friendship to me,
then took that away too quickly
with reasons that, to me, seem trivial
but, to you, means too much.

i can either be wretched enemies, despising your every move;

or just a 'classmate'

i tried the first option, so hard, i tried with until i was drained

that's when the reality hit me, i could never hate you. never.

i love you

and through my love, i accept what you want

"someday i'll get over you"

was what i always used to say

that someday is now,

classmate.

39. Exhale

39. Exhale
The beauty in exhaling
Is one worth experiencing;
Its sort of a sign to bid adieu
To the emotions that swallow you.
Sometimes a little sigh is all it takes
To communicate a thousand words,
To show that one's relieving the multitude.
Breathing out, is a let out to the ones subdued
The power of unspoken words in the air,
Strong enough to make the earth tremble, begins to flare.
But we choose to walk by with an exhale
As we both smile and rejoice with the others,
The mind screams in wonders
If it was at all real,
Or it was all part of an ordeal.
To just smile and exhale, is surreal.
A dying man's exhale concludes his last breath;
While mine concludes yours.

40. Revenge

40. Revenge
revenge.
it feels so sweet
in the pallets of my mind,
to see you regret
and get on knees,
begging me to forget.
unfortunately,
no matter how much time passes,
no matter how much we try
to knit that bond
and rekindle that fire,
I'm not in the least prepared.
in forgetting how you abandoned me,
how you forsook my loyalty,
how you took advantage of my innocence
and burnt it along with your conscience;
how I tried and I tried
but all you did was crucify
time and again
but i never gave up.
I'd fight with you in my mind
during those long showers
when I lost track
whether I was drenched by the water

or my tears.
I won every argument,
I finally made you understand.
but now, a lifetime later,
you speak as if nothing had happened;
like you didn't just prolong my death day by day,
rather brand it as circumstances
that we both went through,
and I'm supposed to welcome you back
with a smile and a hug?
revenge.
or at least a glimpse of it,
is what I can console myself with.
I plot ways to destroy you,
and think of how much I despise you,
all while conversing with you,
with a smile and a hug.

Chapter41

they say when it's destined to be,
a connection sets ablaze like fire,
between two lost souls in searching.
but what do they mean?
they say a friend in need is a friend indeed,
and that nothing will come between;
friends like us who shared roaring laughter.
but what do they really mean?
they say that the ones who stuck through it all
and picked you up from your fall,
can't possibly forget you at all.
but what do they really mean?
but when they said that it's someone who makes you smile,
smile with all your daring might;
a smile that doesn't ring out with anybody else,
a smile that flashes just at the thought of you;
I was sure that they meant you
but you proved it to be untrue.

Chapter42

In the land of black lilies,
I'll take a pink or white maybe.
Black is my favourite,
But I won't put that in my basket,
Since all it seems to bring me is hatred.
I'll leave them all there for once
And let some poor soul pluck them out
To whom I'll unpack my rotten bunch.
To teach, to save
The smudges from my rotten bunch prevail
Yeah that was a hail.
My colourful baskets shine at me
Nevertheless, I don't feel happy.
The black petals hover in my way,
A few get stuck in my hair.
Oh It's calling me to its lair,
Yeah I might as well linger,
Making my heart even darker.

43. Secondary

To say the least, I was heartbroken. In every possible way. However these experiences moulded me into becoming who I am. I can confidently say that I love who I am, for my entirety. Yes I do make mistakes and often get embarrassed and feel like running away. But if the girl who would record herself pointing out the errors in her face, her body, how she loathes herself to her very core, look at who I am now - Someone who loves to see my reflection, someone who actually eats all 3 meals without feeling guilty, someone who keeps trying new things, and is just excited to live life.. Her and I are dimensions apart. Me a year back would be baffled by the things I've achieved now. People who knew me before college often say that they don't recognize me. The way I look may not have changed, but my composure and thoughts have, drastically.
The next 2 poems were written about my insecurity of always being secondary.

43. Secondary

No matter what one can do, or accomplish,

It never seems to replenish.

The hunger to survive,

The hunger to be the best,

The hunger to prove oneself worthy.

No matter how knowledgeable,

Nor the amount of resources one employs,

It will never be enough.

Guess that 'one's' gotta get used to being secondary,

Because no matter how much efforts I put,

That's what I am and will always be,

Secondary.

44. What If we never had Emotions?

44. What If we never had Emotions?

What if we were just mere earthlings?

Not beings filled with hurt, malice and regret;

Just earthlings, whose sole purpose is to exist.

We'd be taken into eternity,

Without a worry;

There'd be no need to hurry nor worry,

There'd be no existence

Of thoughts, words and feelings.

Oh what if this happens!

Just imagine how it'd be!

We'd do our day's work perfectly

Without the consequence of always feeling secondary.

45. Perfection

But let me ask you this question, what is the great deal about being perfect? Perfection is something none can attain. I tried so hard with every bit of my being to be perfect. I wanted to be a high achiever, the best singer, the best looking and so on. Obviously, I failed. Something I've learned is that in life, there will always and always be people who are better than you, and worse than you. I used to be intimidated by those better than me and gloat around those worse than me. Instead, now I've learnt to take things joyfully. Someone's better than me? What a wonderful opportunity to learn! Someone's worse than me? What a wonderful opportunity to teach!
Do whatever you can with the abilities you possess. That is all you need to do. Your best in God's eyes is perfection. Isn't that all that matters? Do your best and leave the rest to God.

45. Perfection

It changes interpretation over time.

But one thing is certain;

None can attain perfection,

Flawlessness, the ultimate

Impossible, even through attempts of infinite.

Why then?

Why must one strive for perfection?

Is it due to narcissism?

Or is it the denial of reality,

That none can achieve supremacy?

Find bliss in yourself,

Feel special in your flaws.

Don't heed the voices of the universe

Enjoy being diverse.

There's only one of you in this world

Why exhaust yourself,

By striving for the impossible?

Nobody's perfect

And that's a comfort.

46. Good Friday

You might've noticed me mentioning God everywhere throughout this book. I wasn't a religious person, until I joined college. College was an eyeopener as to how the world works and each of their lifestyles were quite interesting. In a way, I am thankful to it as it helped me establish my own identity in Christ. The greatest lesson I learnt in my teenage years? God is the only one who will never leave you, and will never stop loving you, no matter how far you've gone. I'm someone who hates change with people in my life. I can't bear losing someone I have now, and I am still coping with people I've lost before. To people like me, God is such a comfort. To know that no matter what, even on my deathbed He'll be there to love me, is the sole reason why I live. To reiterate the previous line, the only reason why I didn't give up my life during any of these years although I wanted to was God. He was my only hope. And always will be.

46. Good Friday

You went on and died for me.

Although you didn't have to be

Murdered in utmost brutality,

And You did it all for me.

Who are you?

The Great I am, The Almighty, The Savior

The Son of the living God, The bread of life, The creator

I could go on,

You would think I'm someone rather exceptional,

Since it seems like a supreme being has died for me.

But who am I?

A speck in the galaxy,

Filled with envy, jealousy.

Yes, I rest with the ugly.

Lesser in importance, compared to a strand of hair;

Worse in character, than a computer in malware;

And yet,

You chose to die for me,

To rise up from the dead for me,

To love, protect me,

Than one possibly could.

He did all of this for me,

Even though I was the reason

For his crucifixion,

But yet he has chosen to give us a mind of our own.

How can I not follow him now?

He did all these things for you too,

Because he loves you so.

Chapter47

Eyes open at the break of dawn,
A cup of coffee a little strong;
This summer seems to go on and on,
But to be back here I'll long.
During fall,
Eyes open to the disastrous call,
The church bells chime for the departed,
Rest in peace cry those abandoned.
The winter will be extra chilly,
Because you're leaving;
Spring often knocks and passes,
Colour flowers spring and die.
But on this tree at calvary,
There was blood shed for me.
It was not in vain,
for the tomb is now left empty.
People say I'm living a fantasy,
If only they knew of the joy in me.
This tree
Has seemed to withstand any storm,
Has braved the throes of thunder,
Has stood by every torn part of me,
Has died for me,
And is the sole reason for my being.
My love for this tree, springs forth due to its consistence,

Due to it always being present.

Where can one find this type of love?

My only wish, is that one day you find it too

And join me with joyous glee!

48. Happy

Finally, I'd like to end this book with my one and only poem I've written about happiness. What is happiness? No just think about it, what is it? Happiness means different things for different people. I thought for a while that having a lot of friends and having good grades is happiness. That later evolved into having a boyfriend. Which later evolved into travelling. The list goes on.

Ironically, when I wrote the poem "Happiness", I had none of what I mentioned above. Happiness struck me when I realised that at the end of the day, everything is going to be okay. No matter what catastrophic event life throws at you, you will figure it out. It might be a mountainous task, but take it step by step and you'll figure it out. To live with the fact that everything will be okay, gave me peace, which resulted in happiness.

48. Happy

The sky looks pink sometimes,

The trees have golden leaves.

The neighbours puppy, a full grown dog,

My handwriting has become pleasing.

My family is just beginning.

Everyday is recovery,

I learnt all this is temporary.

I never thought I'd see myself be happy,

My dependency is on God only.

I started with a dot,

I tried to draw a line.

With every stumble, I grew more,

And now I have a circle,

A loop, that goes on forever,

As the sky and trees change colour.

I realise it doesn't matter,

Even the neighbour's dog has to go on.

I look around and breathe in peace,

Because for once, I'm truly happy.

49. Conclusion

Well, if you've made it thus far, I cannot even bring the words to properly express my gratitude to you. However, I will try. I will try to thank you, by leaving you with a final piece of advice. What is something that would've made my teenage years so much better? And what is something that would help change yours too?

The answer is simple. It's self confidence. I know, I know, you've heard this a million times, and now it just seems so boring. But look at it this way. If I was confident in myself, I would've never let people take advantage of me, so much so that I resent them. A Queen Bee wouldn't have existed, because through my confidence, I'd be my own Queen Bee. I would have never let myself be branded as a speck in the galaxy, I'd call myself the sun. Through the horrifying conflicts, I would've prioritised myself more, and listened to myself more, rather than running around people who did not deserve a minute of my precious time.

Of course there are always dark sides to this. Do not be overconfident. It's a balance, really. Be confident enough to know where you're right and fight for yourself when your conduct is good. But do not be so confident that you are blind to your own mistakes. I implore you to practise this. It's a skill I am new to, but will never stop trying. Standing up for yourself feels so much better than any human being ever doing it for you. When you realise that you have your own support, you'll feel equipped to take over the world. You are never going to leave your side, even if you want to. The relationship between your own self will never end. How about you try to work that one out before you run around others who are temporal anyway?

The only one stopping you from taking over the world is you. No one else.

So what are you waiting for?